101
QUOTES

TO GET YOU THROUGH
THE DAY OR NIGHT

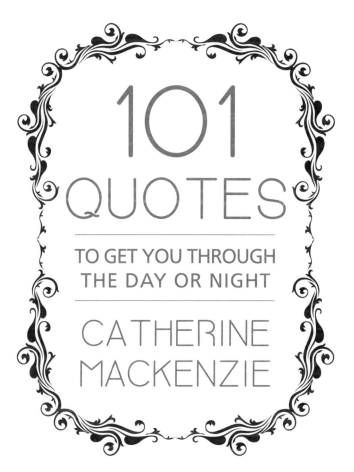

101 QUOTES

TO GET YOU THROUGH THE DAY OR NIGHT

CATHERINE MACKENZIE

CHRISTIAN
FOCUS

10 9 8 7 6 5 4 3 2 1
Copyright © Catherine MacKenzie 2017

ISBN 978-1-78191-889-0

First published in 2017
by Christian Focus Publications Ltd,
Geanies House, Fearn, Ross-shire
IV20 1TW, Scotland
www.christianfocus.com

Unless otherwise stated, Scripture quotations taken from the Holy Bible,
New International Version. Copyright © 1973, 1978, 1984 by Biblica. Used
by permission of Zondervan. All rights reserved.

Scripture quotations are from The Holy Bible, English Standard Version,
copyright © 2001 by Crossway Bibles, a publishing ministry of Good News
Publishers. Used by permission. All rights reserved. ESV Text Edition: 2011.

Scriptures quotations marked KJV are taken from the King James Version
of the Bible.

Scripture verses chosen by Irene Roberts

Designed and typeset by
Pete Barnsley (Creativehoot.com)

Printed and bound by Bell & Bain,
Glasgow

MIX
Paper from
responsible sources
FSC® C007785

CONTENTS

LOVE

"IF WE DO NOT LOVE ONE ANOTHER, WE CERTAINLY SHALL NOT HAVE MUCH POWER WITH GOD IN PRAYER."

D. L. Moody

No one has ever seen God; but if we love one another, God lives in us and his love is made complete in us.

(1 John 4:12)

"HERE IS A CORD OF LOVE LET DOWN, AND THE UPPER END OF IT IS FASTENED TO CHRIST'S HEART, AND THE LOWER END OF IT HANGING DOWN THE LENGTH OF YOUR HEARTS. AND, O! SHALL NOT CHRIST'S HEART AND YOURS BE KNIT TOGETHER THIS DAY? HERE IS A CORD TO BIND HIS HEART TO YOUR HEART, AND YOUR HEART TO HIS HEART."

Ralph Erskine

From him the whole body, joined and held together by every supporting ligament, grows and builds itself up in love, as each part does its work.

(Ephesians 4:16)

"LOVE IS NOT LOVE
WHICH ALTERS WHEN IT
ALTERATION FINDS,
OR BENDS WITH THE REMOVER
TO REMOVE.
NO, IT IS AN EVER-FIXED MARK
THAT LOOKS ON TEMPESTS AND
IS NEVER SHAKEN;
IT IS THE STAR TO EVERY
WAND'RING BARK,
WHOSE WORTH'S UNKNOWN,
ALTHOUGH HIS HEIGHT BE TAKEN."

William Shakespeare

I keep my eyes always on the Lord. With
him at my right hand, I will not be shaken.

(Psalm 16:8)

"TRUE LOVE'S THE GIFT THAT GOD
  HAS GIVEN
TO MAN ALONE BENEATH THE
HEAVENS
IT IS NOT FANTASY'S HOT FIRE
WHOSE WISHES, AS SOON AS
  GRANT'D, FLY
IT LIVETH NOT IN FIERCE DESIRE
WITH DESIRE DEAD, IT DOES NOT DIE
IT IS THE SECRET SYMPATHY,
THE SILVER LINK – THE SILKEN TIE
WHICH HEART TO HEART AND MIND
  TO MIND
IN BODY AND IN SOUL CAN BIND."

Walter Scott

If I have the gift of prophecy and can fathom all mysteries and all knowledge, and if I have a faith that can move mountains, but do not have love, I am nothing.

(1 Corinthians 13:2)

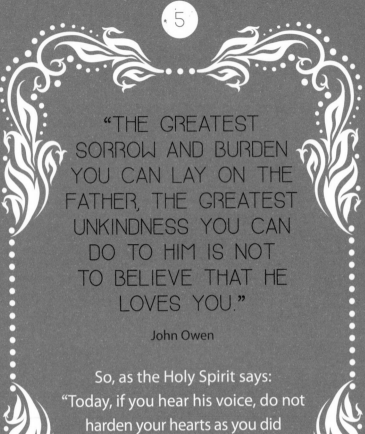

"THE GREATEST SORROW AND BURDEN YOU CAN LAY ON THE FATHER, THE GREATEST UNKINDNESS YOU CAN DO TO HIM IS NOT TO BELIEVE THAT HE LOVES YOU."

John Owen

So, as the Holy Spirit says:
"Today, if you hear his voice, do not harden your hearts as you did in the rebellion, during the time of testing in the wilderness."

(Hebrews 3:7-8)

"THERE IS TREMENDOUS RELIEF IN KNOWING HIS LOVE TO ME IS UTTERLY REALISTIC, BASED AT EVERY POINT ON PRIOR KNOWLEDGE OF THE WORST ABOUT ME, SO THAT NO DISCOVERY CAN DISILLUSION HIM ABOUT ME, IN THE WAY I AM SO OFTEN DISILLUSIONED ABOUT MYSELF, AND QUENCH HIS DETERMINATION TO BLESS ME."

J.I. Packer

You have searched me, LORD, and you know me. You know when I sit and when I rise; you perceive my thoughts from afar.

(Psalm 139:1-2)

"THE FAILURE OF MANY IS TO SEEK FROM MAN WHAT CAN BE FOUND ONLY IN GOD. ALL HUMAN AFFECTION IS EMPTY; THE LOVE OF GOD ALONE IS ABLE TO FULLY SATISFY ONE'S DESIRE. THE MOMENT A CHRISTIAN SEEKS A LOVE OUTSIDE GOD HIS SPIRITUAL LIFE IMMEDIATELY FALLS."

Watchman Nee

He will call on me, and I will answer him; I will be with him in trouble, I will deliver him and honour him. With long life I will satisfy him and show him my salvation.

(Psalm 91:15-16)

"I BELIEVE THAT MUCH OF THE SECRET OF SOUL-WINNING LIES IN HAVING BOWELS OF COMPASSION, IN HAVING SPIRITS THAT CAN BE TOUCHED WITH THE FEELING OF HUMAN INFIRMITIES."

Charles Spurgeon

Therefore if you have any encouragement from being united with Christ, if any comfort from his love, if any common sharing in the Spirit, if any tenderness and compassion, then make my joy complete by being like-minded, having the same love, being one in spirit and of one mind. Do nothing out of selfish ambition or vain conceit. Rather, in humility value others above yourselves.

(Philippians 2:1-3)

"OUR LOVE GROWS SOFT IF IT IS NOT STRENGTHENED BY TRUTH, AND OUR TRUTH GROWS HARD IF IT IS NOT SOFTENED BY LOVE."

John Stott

Instead, speaking the truth in love, we will grow to become in every respect the mature body of him who is the head, that is, Christ.

(Ephesians 4:15)

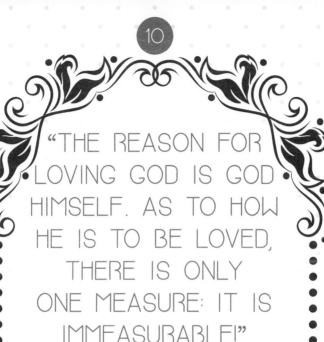

"THE REASON FOR LOVING GOD IS GOD HIMSELF. AS TO HOW HE IS TO BE LOVED, THERE IS ONLY ONE MEASURE: IT IS IMMEASURABLE!"

Bernard of Clairvaux

Jesus replied, "Love the Lord your God with all your heart and with all your soul and with all your mind."

(Matthew 22:37)

"OUR FORGIVING LOVE TOWARD MEN IS THE EVIDENCE OF GOD'S FORGIVING LOVE IN US. IT IS A NECESSARY CONDITION OF THE PRAYER OF FAITH."

Andrew Murray

For if you forgive other people when they sin against you, your heavenly Father will also forgive you. But if you do not forgive others their sins, your Father will not forgive your sins.

(Matthew 6:14-15)

"WHEN I HAVE LEARNT TO LOVE GOD BETTER THAN MY EARTHLY DEAREST, I SHALL LOVE MY EARTHLY DEAREST BETTER THAN I DO NOW."

C. S. Lewis

Anyone who loves their father or mother more than me is not worthy of me; anyone who loves their son or daughter more than me is not worthy of me.

(Matthew 10:37)

"I BECAME MY OWN ONLY WHEN I GAVE MYSELF TO ANOTHER."

C. S. Lewis

Be devoted to one another in love. Honour one another above yourselves.

(Romans 12:10)

"LOVE ALWAYS INVOLVES RESPONSIBILITY, AND LOVE ALWAYS INVOLVES SACRIFICE. AND WE DO NOT REALLY LOVE CHRIST UNLESS WE ARE PREPARED TO FACE HIS TASK AND TO TAKE UP HIS CROSS."

William Barclay

Then Jesus said to his disciples, "Whoever wants to be my disciple must deny themselves and take up their cross and follow me."

(Matthew 16:24)

"DO NOT WASTE TIME BOTHERING WHETHER YOU 'LOVE' YOUR NEIGHBOUR; ACT AS IF YOU DID."

C. S. Lewis

"Teacher, which is the greatest commandment in the Law?"
Jesus replied: "'Love the Lord your God with all your heart and with all your soul and with all your mind.' This is the first and greatest commandment. And the second is like it: 'Love your neighbour as yourself.'"

(Matthew 22:36-39)

"THE MORE YOU LEAD ME UP TO CHRIST IN ALL THINGS, THE MORE HIGHLY SHALL I ESTEEM YOU, AND IF IT BE POSSIBLE TO LOVE YOU MORE THAN I DO NOW, THE MORE SHALL I LOVE YOU."

Catherine Booth

"A new command I give you: Love one another. As I have loved you, so you must love one another. By this everyone will know that you are my disciples, if you love one another."

(John 13:34-35)

"THE BIBLE TELLS
US TO LOVE OUR
NEIGHBOURS, AND ALSO
TO LOVE OUR ENEMIES:
PROBABLY BECAUSE
THEY ARE GENERALLY
THE SAME PEOPLE."

G. K. Chesterton

"But to you who are listening I say: Love
your enemies, do good to those who hate
you, bless those who curse you, pray for
those who mistreat you."

(Luke 6:27-28)

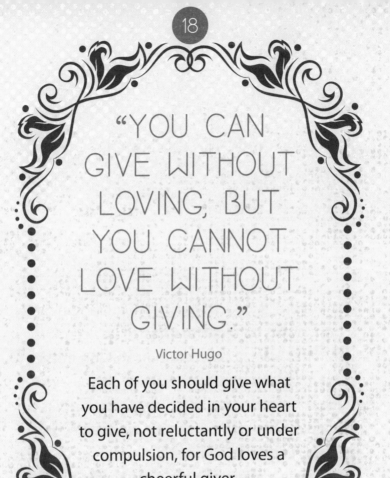

"YOU CAN GIVE WITHOUT LOVING, BUT YOU CANNOT LOVE WITHOUT GIVING."

Victor Hugo

Each of you should give what you have decided in your heart to give, not reluctantly or under compulsion, for God loves a cheerful giver.

(2 Corinthians 9:7)

"THE POOREST AND MOST IGNORANT CHRISTIAN CAN EVERY DAY FIND OCCASION FOR PRACTICING LOVE AND HUMILITY."

J. C. Ryle

Therefore if you have any encouragement from being united with Christ, if any comfort from his love, if any common sharing in the Spirit, if any tenderness and compassion, then make my joy complete by being like-minded, having the same love, being one in spirit and of one mind. Do nothing out of selfish ambition or vain conceit. Rather, in humility value others above yourselves.

(Philippians 2:1-3)

"BEWARE YOU ARE NOT SWALLOWED UP IN BOOKS! AN OUNCE OF LOVE IS WORTH A POUND OF KNOWLEDGE."

John Wesley

And this is my prayer: that your love may abound more and more in knowledge and depth of insight.

(Philippians 1:9)

"LOVE IS THE SUM OF ALL VIRTUE, AND LOVE DISPOSES US TO GOOD."

Jonathan Edwards

Therefore, as God's chosen people, holy and dearly loved, clothe yourselves with compassion, kindness, humility, gentleness and patience. Bear with each other and forgive one another if any of you has a grievance against someone. Forgive as the Lord forgave you. And over all these virtues put on love, which binds them all together in perfect unity.

(Colossians 3:12-14)

"NO MAN LOVETH GOD EXCEPT THE MAN WHO HAS FIRST LEARNED THAT GOD LOVES HIM."

Alexander MacLaren

No, the Father himself loves you because you have loved me and have believed that I came from God.

(John 16:27)

"LOVE CANNOT THINK ANY EVIL OF GOD, NOR ENDURE TO HEAR ANY SPEAK EVIL OF HIM, BUT IT MUST TAKE GOD'S PART."

William Gurnall

Love is patient, love is kind. It does not envy, it does not boast, it is not proud. It does not dishonour others, it is not self-seeking, it is not easily angered, it keeps no record of wrongs.

(1 Corinthians 13:4-5)

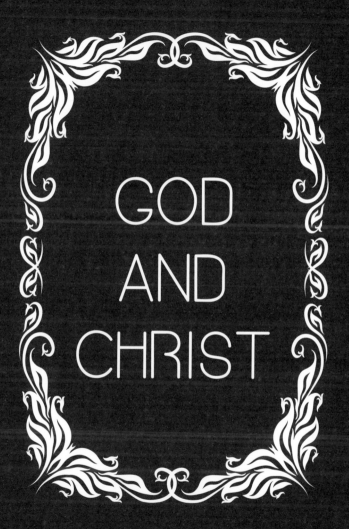

GOD
AND
CHRIST

24

"HISTORIC FIGURES HAVE HOMES TO VISIT FOR POSTERITY; THE LORD OF HISTORY LEFT NO HOME. LUMINARIES LEAVE LIBRARIES AND WRITE THEIR MEMOIRS; HE LEFT ONE BOOK, PENNED BY ORDINARY PEOPLE. DELIVERERS SPEAK OF WINNING THROUGH MIGHT AND CONQUEST; HE SPOKE OF A PLACE IN THE HEART."

Ravi Zacharias

Jesus replied, "Foxes have dens and birds have nests, but the Son of Man has no place to lay his head."

(Luke 9:58)

"OUR GOD, OUR HELP IN AGES PAST,
OUR HOPE FOR YEARS TO COME,
OUR SHELTER FROM THE STORMY BLAST,
AND OUR ETERNAL HOME."

Isaac Watts

Lord, you have been our dwelling place
Throughout all generations.
Before the mountains were born
Or you brought forth the whole world,
From everlasting to everlasting you
are God.

(Psalm 90:1)

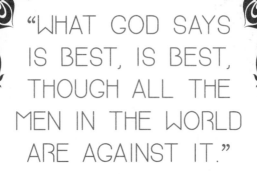

"WHAT GOD SAYS
IS BEST, IS BEST,
THOUGH ALL THE
MEN IN THE WORLD
ARE AGAINST IT."

John Bunyan

This is what the Lord says — your
Redeemer, the Holy One of Israel:
"I am the Lord your God, who
teaches you what is best for you,
who directs you in the way you
should go."

(Isaiah 48:17)

"WE WILL NEVER COME TO KNOW THE LORD JESUS CHRIST AS A REALITY UNTIL WE SEE HIM AS A NECESSITY."

Alistair Begg

"For it is by grace you have been saved, through faith—and this is not from yourselves, it is the gift of God—not by works, so that no one can boast."

(Ephesians 2:8-9)

"BELIEVE THAT CHRIST DIED FOR YOU. HE SUFFERED FOR YOU. HE WON THE BATTLE OVER SIN FOR YOU. HE ROSE FROM THE GRAVE AND WAS VICTORIOUS OVER DEATH SO THAT YOU CAN LIVE FOREVER."

Billy Graham

For God so loved the world that he gave his one and only Son, that whoever believes in him shall not perish but have eternal life.

(John 3:16)

"THERE IS A GOD IN HEAVEN WHO OVERRULES ALL THINGS FOR THE BEST; AND THIS IS THE COMFORT OF MY SOUL ... HOW BLESSED IT IS TO GROW MORE AND MORE LIKE GOD!"

David Brainerd

The LORD has established his throne in heaven, and his kingdom rules over all.

(Psalm 103:19)

"WHAT THINK WE OF CHRIST? IS HE ALTOGETHER GLORIOUS IN OUR EYES, AND PRECIOUS TO OUR HEARTS? MAY CHRIST BE OUR JOY, OUR CONFIDENCE, OUR ALL. MAY WE DAILY BE MADE MORE LIKE TO HIM, AND MORE DEVOTED TO HIS SERVICE."

Matthew Henry

Instead, speaking the truth in love, we will grow to become in every respect the mature body of him who is the head, that is, Christ.

(Ephesians 4:15)

"WHAT WE NEED TO KNOW ABOUT HEAVEN IS NOT SO MUCH WHERE IT IS, BUT WHO IS THERE. HEAVEN IS WHERE MY SAVIOR IS. HEAVEN IS WHERE THE ONE WHO HAS SAVED ME AND THE ONE IN WHOM I DELIGHT DWELLS. THEREFORE, I REALLY DO NOT CARE WHERE HEAVEN IS LOCATED, AS LONG AS I AM THERE WITH HIM AND WITH ALL OF THOSE WHO LOVE HIM."

Ligon Duncan

I tell you, my friends, do not be afraid of those who kill the body and after that can do no more.

(Luke 12:4)

SALVATION

"I AM NOT THE MAN I OUGHT TO BE, I AM NOT THE MAN I WISH TO BE, AND I AM NOT THE MAN I HOPE TO BE, BUT BY THE GRACE OF GOD, I AM NOT THE MAN I USED TO BE."

John Newton

For I have the desire to do what is good, but I cannot carry it out. For I do not do the good I want to do, but the evil I do not want to do—this I keep on doing. Now if I do what I do not want to do, it is no longer I who do it, but it is sin living in me that does it.

(Romans 7:18-20)

"... CHRIST'S SALVATION MUST BE A FREE GIFT. HE 'PURCHASED' IT FOR US AT THE HIGH PRICE OF HIS OWN LIFE-BLOOD. SO WHAT IS THERE LEFT FOR US TO PAY? NOTHING! SINCE HE CLAIMED THAT ALL WAS NOW 'FINISHED', THERE IS NOTHING FOR US TO CONTRIBUTE."

John Stott

He did not enter by means of the blood of goats and calves; but he entered the Most Holy Place once for all by his own blood, thus obtaining eternal redemption.

(Hebrews 9:12)

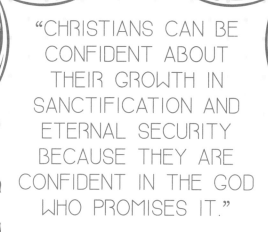

"CHRISTIANS CAN BE CONFIDENT ABOUT THEIR GROWTH IN SANCTIFICATION AND ETERNAL SECURITY BECAUSE THEY ARE CONFIDENT IN THE GOD WHO PROMISES IT."

John Owen

And that is what some of you were. But you were washed, you were sanctified, you were justified in the name of the Lord Jesus Christ and by the Spirit of our God.

(1 Corinthians 6:11)

"HE IS NO FOOL WHO PARTS WITH THAT WHICH HE CANNOT KEEP, WHEN HE IS SURE TO BE RECOMPENSED WITH THAT WHICH HE CANNOT LOSE."

Philip Henry

In everything I did, I showed you that by this kind of hard work we must help the weak, remembering the words the Lord Jesus himself said: "It is more blessed to give than to receive."

(Acts 20:35)

"THERE IS NO WAY UNDER HEAVEN TO BE INTERESTED IN CHRIST, BUT BY BELIEVING. HE THAT BELIEVETH SHALL BE SAVED, LET HIS SINS, BE EVER SO GREAT; AND HE THAT BELIEVETH NOT SHALL BE DAMNED, LET HIS SINS BE EVER SO LITTLE."

Thomas Brooks

If you declare with your mouth, "Jesus is Lord", and believe in your heart that God raised him from the dead, you will be saved.

(Romans 10:9)

"AS THE EARLY CHURCH FATHERS DELIGHTED IN SAYING, CHRIST TOOK WHAT WAS OURS SO THAT WE MIGHT RECEIVE WHAT WAS HIS."

Sinclair B. Ferguson

But when the set time had fully come, God sent his Son, born of a woman, born under the law, to redeem those under the law, that we might receive adoption to sonship.

(Galatians 4:4-5)

"YOUR APPROVAL BEFORE GOD IS WOVEN INTO THE LIFE AND SACRIFICE OF JESUS CHRIST ON THE CROSS, NOT WHAT OTHER MEN AND WOMEN THINK ABOUT YOU."

Matt Chandler

Do your best to present yourself to God as one approved, a worker who does not need to be ashamed and who correctly handles the word of truth.

(2 Timothy 2:15)

SALVATION  41

"IF YOU SHOULD SEE A MAN SHUT UP IN A CLOSED ROOM, IDOLIZING A SET OF LAMPS AND REJOICING IN THEIR LIGHT, AND YOU WISHED TO MAKE HIM TRULY HAPPY, YOU WOULD BEGIN BY BLOWING OUT ALL HIS LAMPS; AND THEN THROW OPEN THE SHUTTERS TO LET IN THE LIGHT OF HEAVEN."

Samuel Rutherford

'Do not make idols or set up an image or a sacred stone for yourselves, and do not place a carved stone in your land to bow down before it. I am the LORD your God.'

(Leviticus 26:1)

SALVATION

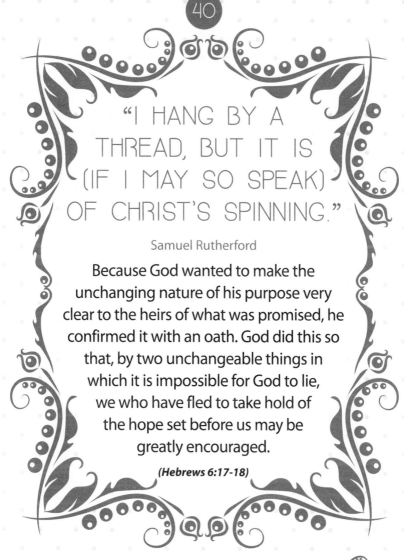

"I HANG BY A THREAD, BUT IT IS (IF I MAY SO SPEAK) OF CHRIST'S SPINNING."

Samuel Rutherford

Because God wanted to make the unchanging nature of his purpose very clear to the heirs of what was promised, he confirmed it with an oath. God did this so that, by two unchangeable things in which it is impossible for God to lie, we who have fled to take hold of the hope set before us may be greatly encouraged.

(Hebrews 6:17-18)

"WE CAN EXAMINE OURSELVES IN THE LIGHT OF SCRIPTURE, AND IF WE DO THAT WE SHALL BE DRIVEN TO CHRIST. BUT WITH INTROSPECTION A MAN LOOKS AT HIMSELF AND CONTINUES TO DO SO, AND REFUSES TO BE HAPPY UNTIL HE GETS RID OF THE IMPERFECTIONS THAT ARE STILL THERE. OH, THE TRAGEDY THAT WE SHOULD SPEND OUR LIVES LOOKING AT OURSELVES INSTEAD OF LOOKING AT HIM WHO CAN SET US FREE!"

Martyn Lloyd-Jones

Do nothing out of selfish ambition or vain conceit. Rather, in humility value others above yourselves, not looking to your own interests but each of you to the interests of the others. In your relationships with one another, have the same mindset as Christ Jesus.

(Philippians 2:3-5)

"IF WE BELIEVE THAT JESUS OF NAZARETH IS THE ONLY BEGOTTEN SON OF GOD AND THAT HE CAME INTO THIS WORLD AND WENT TO THE CROSS OF CALVARY AND DIED FOR OUR SINS AND ROSE AGAIN IN ORDER TO JUSTIFY US AND TO GIVE US LIFE ANEW AND PREPARE US FOR HEAVEN–IF YOU REALLY BELIEVE THAT, THERE IS ONLY ONE INEVITABLE DEDUCTION, NAMELY THAT HE IS ENTITLED TO THE WHOLE OF OUR LIVES, WITHOUT ANY LIMIT WHATSOEVER."

Martyn Lloyd-Jones

For what I received I passed on to you as of first importance: that Christ died for our sins according to the Scriptures, that he was buried, that he was raised on the third day according to the Scriptures, and that he appeared to Cephas, and then to the Twelve.

(1 Corinthians 15:3-5)

43

"THE TERRIBLE, TRAGIC FALLACY OF THE LAST HUNDRED YEARS HAS BEEN TO THINK THAT ALL MAN'S TROUBLES ARE DUE TO HIS ENVIRONMENT, AND THAT TO CHANGE THE MAN YOU HAVE NOTHING TO DO BUT CHANGE HIS ENVIRONMENT. THAT IS A TRAGIC FALLACY. IT OVERLOOKS THE FACT THAT IT WAS IN PARADISE THAT MAN FELL."

Martyn Lloyd-Jones

Therefore, just as sin entered the world through one man, and death through sin, and in this way death came to all people, because all sinned.

(Romans 5:12)

46 SALVATION

"GOD'S GIFTS
PUT MAN'S
BEST DREAMS
TO SHAME."

Elizabeth Barrett Browning

… for God's gifts and his call are
irrevocable.

(Romans 11:29)

PRAYER

"I AM PROFOUNDLY GRATEFUL TO GOD THAT HE DID NOT GRANT ME CERTAIN THINGS FOR WHICH I ASKED, AND THAT HE SHUT CERTAIN DOORS IN MY FACE."

Martyn Lloyd-Jones

When you ask, you do not receive, because you ask with wrong motives, that you may spend what you get on your pleasures.

(James 4:3)

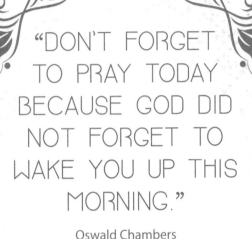

"DON'T FORGET TO PRAY TODAY BECAUSE GOD DID NOT FORGET TO WAKE YOU UP THIS MORNING."

Oswald Chambers

My heart says of you,
"Seek his face!" Your face,
LORD, I will seek.

(Psalm 27:8)

"PRAYER DOES CHANGE THINGS, ALL KINDS OF THINGS. BUT THE MOST IMPORTANT THING IT CHANGES IS US. AS WE ENGAGE IN THIS COMMUNION WITH GOD MORE DEEPLY AND COME TO KNOW THE ONE WITH WHOM WE ARE SPEAKING MORE INTIMATELY, THAT GROWING KNOWLEDGE OF GOD REVEALS TO US ALL THE MORE BRILLIANTLY WHO WE ARE AND OUR NEED TO CHANGE IN CONFORMITY TO HIM. PRAYER CHANGES US PROFOUNDLY."

R.C. Sproul

Therefore I tell you, whatever you ask for in prayer, believe that you have received it, and it will be yours.

(Mark 11:24)

"A TINGLING SENSE OF
EXPECTANCY CHARACTERISES
THE CHURCH THAT PRAYS.
CHURCH WORSHIP, FELLOWSHIP
AND OUTREACH BECOME
IRRADIATED WITH THE
PRESENCE AND POWER OF
CHRIST HIMSELF WHEN PRAYER
IS RECOGNISED AS THE MOST
IMPORTANT ACTIVITY OF ALL!"

Richard Bewes

Rejoice in hope, be patient
in tribulation, be constant
in prayer.

(Romans 12:12 ESV)

P316 Penmon Lighthouse and Puffin Island
Goleudy Penmon ag Ynys Seiriol

© Dave Newbould — 01341 241538,   www.origins-photography.co.uk

ORIGINS
GWREIDDIAU

Snowdonia Design & Print • Porthmadog

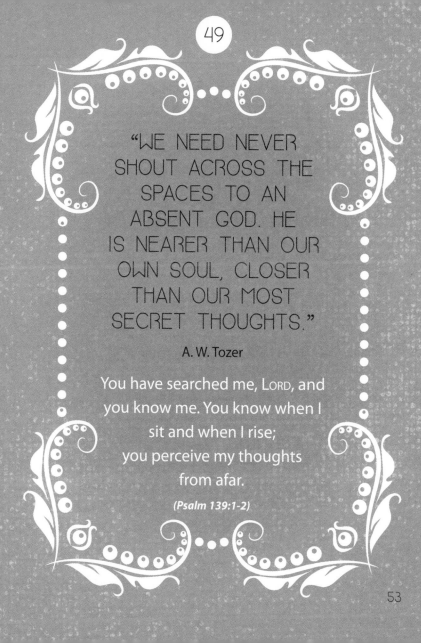

"WE NEED NEVER SHOUT ACROSS THE SPACES TO AN ABSENT GOD. HE IS NEARER THAN OUR OWN SOUL, CLOSER THAN OUR MOST SECRET THOUGHTS."

A. W. Tozer

You have searched me, LORD, and you know me. You know when I sit and when I rise; you perceive my thoughts from afar.

(Psalm 139:1-2)

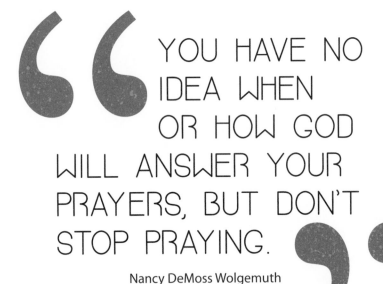

YOU HAVE NO IDEA WHEN OR HOW GOD WILL ANSWER YOUR PRAYERS, BUT DON'T STOP PRAYING.

Nancy DeMoss Wolgemuth

Rejoice always, pray continually, give thanks in all circumstances; for this is God's will for you in Christ Jesus.

(1 Thessalonians 5:16-18)

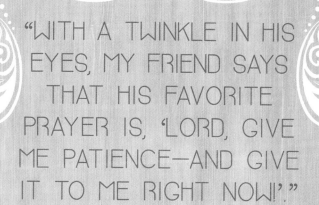

"WITH A TWINKLE IN HIS EYES, MY FRIEND SAYS THAT HIS FAVORITE PRAYER IS, 'LORD, GIVE ME PATIENCE—AND GIVE IT TO ME RIGHT NOW!'."

Billy Graham

My brethren, count it all joy when ye fall into divers temptations; Knowing this, that the trying of your faith worketh patience. But let patience have her perfect work, that ye may be perfect and entire, wanting nothing.

(James 1:2-4 KJV)

"LET THE FIRST MOMENTS OF THE DAY, WHEN THE HEART IS FRESH, BE GIVEN TO GOD. NEVER SEE THE FACE OF MAN UNTIL YOU HAVE SEEN THE KING. DARE TO BE ALONE OFTEN ON THE MOUNT."

F.B. Meyer

In the morning, LORD, you hear my voice; in the morning I lay my requests before you and wait expectantly.

(Psalm 5:3)

"THE SOUL WHICH HAS COME INTO INTIMATE CONTACT WITH GOD IN THE SILENCE OF THE PRAYER CHAMBER IS NEVER OUT OF CONSCIOUS TOUCH WITH THE FATHER, THE HEART IS ALWAYS GOING OUT TO HIM IN LOVING COMMUNION, AND THE MOMENT THE MIND IS RELEASED FROM THE TASK UPON WHICH IT IS ENGAGED, IT RETURNS AS NATURALLY TO GOD AS THE BIRD DOES TO ITS NEST."

E. M. Bounds

The glory that you have given me I have given to them, that they may be one even as we are one, I in them and you in me, that they may become perfectly one, so that the world may know that you sent me and loved them even as you loved me.

(John 17:22-23 ESV)

"WE NEED GOD IN WAYS WE DO NOT KNOW. DON'T LIMIT YOUR EXPERIENCE OF GOD TO WHAT YOU CAN THINK TO ASK. ASK FOR THE UNKNOWN JOY."

John Piper

Until now you have not asked for anything in my name. Ask and you will receive, and your joy will be complete.

(John 16:24)

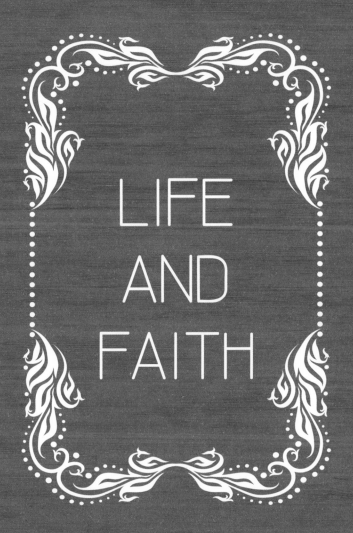

LIFE
AND
FAITH

"IF YOU DON'T FEEL STRONG DESIRES FOR THE MANIFESTATION OF THE GLORY OF GOD, IT IS NOT BECAUSE YOU HAVE DRUNK DEEPLY AND ARE SATISFIED. IT IS BECAUSE YOU HAVE NIBBLED SO LONG AT THE TABLE OF THE WORLD. YOUR SOUL IS STUFFED WITH SMALL THINGS, AND THERE IS NO ROOM FOR THE GREAT. GOD DID NOT CREATE YOU FOR THIS."

John Piper

Blessed are those who hunger and thirst for righteousness, for they will be filled.

(Matthew 5:6)

 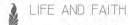

"THE POOREST PLOUGHMAN IS IN CHRIST EQUAL WITH THE GREATEST PRINCE THAT IS. LET THEM THEREFORE HAVE SUFFICIENT TO MAINTAIN THEM ..."

Hugh Latimer

Is he not the One who ... shows no partiality to princes and does not favor the rich over the poor, for they are all the work of his hands,

(Job 34:18-19)

"THIS HILL, THOUGH HIGH, I
COVET TO ASCEND;
THE DIFFICULTY WILL NOT ME
OFFEND.
FOR I PERCEIVE THE WAY TO
LIFE LIES HERE.
COME, PLUCK UP, HEART; LET'S
NEITHER FAINT NOR FEAR.
BETTER, THOUGH DIFFICULT,
THE RIGHT WAY TO GO,
THAN WRONG, THOUGH EASY,
WHERE THE END IS WOE."

John Bunyan

"Enter through the narrow gate. For wide is
the gate and broad is the road that leads to
destruction, and many enter through it."

(Matthew 7:13)

  LIFE AND FAITH

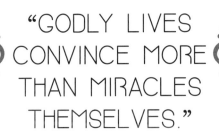

"GODLY LIVES CONVINCE MORE THAN MIRACLES THEMSELVES."

Thomas Brooks

His divine power has given us
everything we need for a godly life
through our knowledge of
him who called us by his own
glory and goodness.

(2 Peter 1:3)

"YOUR LOVES
SHOW WHAT YOU
ACTUALLY BELIEVE
IN, NOT WHAT YOU
SAY YOU DO."

Timothy Keller

But as it is written, Eye hath not seen,
nor ear heard, neither have entered into
the heart of man, the things which
God hath prepared for them
that love him.

(1 Corinthians 2:9 KJV)

"I HAVE LEARNED THAT IN EVERY CIRCUMSTANCE THAT COMES MY WAY, I CAN CHOOSE TO RESPOND IN ONE OF TWO WAYS: I CAN WHINE OR I CAN WORSHIP! AND I CAN'T WORSHIP WITHOUT GIVING THANKS. IT JUST ISN'T POSSIBLE. WHEN WE CHOOSE THE PATHWAY OF WORSHIP AND GIVING THANKS, ESPECIALLY IN THE MIDST OF DIFFICULT CIRCUMSTANCES, THERE IS A FRAGRANCE, A RADIANCE, THAT ISSUES FORTH OUT OF OUR LIVES TO BLESS THE LORD AND OTHERS."

Nancy DeMoss Wolgemuth

For we are to God the pleasing aroma of Christ among those who are being saved and those who are perishing.

(2 Corinthians 2:15)

"INSTEAD OF A RIVER, GOD OFTEN GIVES US A BROOK, WHICH MAY BE RUNNING TODAY AND DRIED UP TOMORROW. WHY? TO TEACH US NOT TO REST IN OUR BLESSINGS, BUT IN THE BLESSER HIMSELF."

Arthur W. Pink

Truly my soul finds rest in God; my salvation comes from him.

(Psalm 62:1)

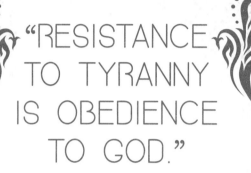

"RESISTANCE TO TYRANNY IS OBEDIENCE TO GOD."

John Knox

Observe the commands of
the LORD your God, walking
in obedience to him and
revering him.

(Deuteronomy 8:6)

"FAITH DOES NOT ELIMINATE QUESTIONS. BUT FAITH KNOWS WHERE TO TAKE THEM."

Elisabeth Elliot

"Because you have so little faith. Truly I tell you, if you have faith as small as a mustard seed, you can say to this mountain, 'Move from here to there,' and it will move. Nothing will be impossible for you."

(Matthew 17:20)

"CHRISTIAN PATRIOTS SPEND MORE TIME WASHING FEET THAN WAVING FLAGS."

Charles W. Colson

Now that I, your Lord and
Teacher, have washed your feet,
you also should wash
one another's feet.

(John 13:14)

"THAT WHICH MAN BUILDS MAN DESTROYS, BUT THE CITY OF GOD IS BUILT BY GOD AND CANNOT BE DESTROYED BY MAN."

Augustine of Hippo

For we know that if the earthly tent we live in is destroyed, we have a building from God, an eternal house in heaven, not built by human hands.

(2 Corinthians 5:1)

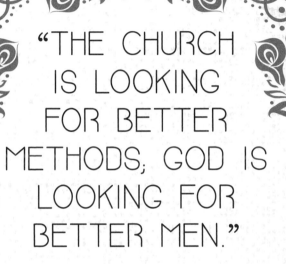

"THE CHURCH IS LOOKING FOR BETTER METHODS; GOD IS LOOKING FOR BETTER MEN."

E. M. Bounds

God made him who had no sin to be sin for us, so that in him we might become the righteousness of God.

(2 Corinthians 5:21)

"IF WE WOULD MEND
THE WORLD,
WE SHOULD MEND
OURSELVES;
AND TEACH OUR
CHILDREN TO BE,
NOT WHAT WE ARE,
BUT WHAT THEY
SHOULD BE."

William Penn

Only be careful, and watch yourselves closely so that you do not forget the things your eyes have seen or let them fade from your heart as long as you live. Teach them to your children and to their children after them.

(Deuteronomy 4:9)

"FEELINGS COME AND FEELINGS GO,
AND FEELINGS ARE DECEIVING;
MY WARRANT IS THE WORD OF GOD—
NAUGHT ELSE IS WORTH BELIEVING.

THOUGH ALL MY HEART SHOULD FEEL
  CONDEMNED
FOR WANT OF SOME SWEET TOKEN,
THERE IS ONE GREATER THAN MY HEART
WHOSE WORD CANNOT BE BROKEN.

I'LL TRUST IN GOD'S UNCHANGING WORD
TILL SOUL AND BODY SEVER,
FOR, THOUGH ALL THINGS SHALL
  PASS AWAY,
HIS WORD SHALL STAND FOREVER!"

Martin Luther

The grass withers, the flower fades, but the word of our God will stand forever.

(Isaiah 40:8 ESV)

"I KNEEL BEFORE YOU,
JESUS, CRUCIFIED,
MY CROSS IS
SHOULDERED AND MY
SELF DENIED;
I'LL FOLLOW DAILY,
CLOSELY, NOT REFUSE
FOR LOVE OF YOU AND
MAN MYSELF TO LOSE."

John Stott

Then he said to them all: "Whoever wants to be my disciple must deny themselves and take up their cross daily and follow me."

(Luke 9:23)

"THE SECRET TO HAPPINESS IS FOUND IN OBEDIENCE TO GOD. HOW CAN WE BE HAPPY IF WE ARE NOT OBEDIENT? HOW CAN WE BE OBEDIENT IF WE DO NOT KNOW WHAT IT IS WE ARE TO OBEY? THUS THE TOP AND THE TAIL OF IT IS THAT HAPPINESS CANNOT BE FULLY DISCOVERED AS LONG AS WE REMAIN IGNORANT OF GOD'S WORD."

R.C. Sproul

Obey me, and I will be your God and you will be my people. Walk in obedience to all I command you, that it may go well with you.

(Jeremiah 7:23)

"I DO NOT CONSECRATE MYSELF TO BE A MISSIONARY OR A PREACHER. I CONSECRATE MYSELF TO GOD TO DO HIS WILL WHERE I AM, BE IT IN SCHOOL, OFFICE, OR KITCHEN, OR WHEREVER HE MAY, IN HIS WISDOM, SEND ME."

Watchman Nee

"Consecrate yourselves and be holy, because I am the LORD your God."

(Leviticus 20:7)

"IT IS SO EASY TO
BECOME MORE
ATTACHED TO THE
GIFTS OF GOD THAN
TO THE GIVER—AND
EVEN, I SHOULD ADD, TO
THE WORK OF GOD THAN
TO GOD HIMSELF."

Watchman Nee

Not that I desire your gifts;
what I desire is that more
be credited to your account.

(Philippians 4:17)

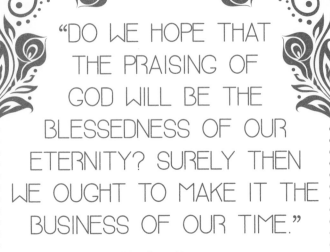

"DO WE HOPE THAT THE PRAISING OF GOD WILL BE THE BLESSEDNESS OF OUR ETERNITY? SURELY THEN WE OUGHT TO MAKE IT THE BUSINESS OF OUR TIME."

Matthew Henry

Surely your goodness and love will follow me all the days of my life, and I will dwell in the house of the LORD forever.

(Psalm 23:6)

SUFFERING, COMFORT AND CONTENTMENT

"HE HAS CHOSEN
NOT TO HEAL ME,
BUT TO HOLD ME.
THE MORE
INTENSE THE PAIN,
THE CLOSER
HIS EMBRACE."

Joni Eareckson Tada

He reached down from on high
and took hold of me; he drew me
out of deep waters.

(Psalm 18:16)

"THE GOOD MAN, THOUGH A SLAVE, IS FREE; THE WICKED, THOUGH HE REIGNS, IS A SLAVE, AND NOT THE SLAVE OF A SINGLE MAN, BUT — WHAT IS WORSE — THE SLAVE OF AS MANY MASTERS AS HE HAS VICES."

Augustine of Hippo

"Come to me, all you who are weary and burdened, and I will give you rest."

(Matthew 11:28)

"YOU HAVE MADE US FOR YOURSELF, O LORD, AND OUR HEARTS ARE RESTLESS UNTIL THEY REST IN YOU."

Augustine of Hippo

Truly my soul finds rest in God; my salvation comes from him.

(Psalm 62:1)

SUFFERING, COMFORT AND CONTENTMENT

"TEARS SHED
FOR SELF ARE
TEARS OF
WEAKNESS, BUT
TEARS SHED
FOR OTHERS
ARE A SIGN OF
STRENGTH."

Billy Graham

Carry each other's burdens, and in this
way you will fulfill the law of Christ.

(Galatians 6:2)

"YES, MY MASTER IS THOROUGH. HE WOUNDS, BUT HE BINDS UP, AND HIS BALM OF GILEAD HEALS WITHOUT STINGING; IT COOLS, REFRESHES, AND RESTORES IN EVERY PART. HE GIVES THE GARMENT OF PRAISE FOR THE SPIRIT OF HEAVINESS, AND BRINGS BEAUTY OUT OF OUR ASHES."

Isobel Kuhn

… and provide for those who grieve in Zion—to bestow on them a crown of beauty instead of ashes, the oil of joy instead of mourning, and a garment of praise instead of a spirit of despair.

(Isaiah 61:3)

"WHERE
IS GOD IN
SUFFERING?
HE'S IN IT WITH US,
AND IN IT FOR US."

Thabiti M. Anyabwile

Surely he took up our pain and
bore our suffering, yet we
considered him punished by God,
stricken by him, and afflicted.

(Isaiah 53:4)

"GRATITUDE UNLEASHES THE FREEDOM TO LIVE CONTENT IN THE MOMENT, RATHER THAN BEING ANXIOUS ABOUT THE FUTURE OR REGRETTING THE PAST."

Nancy DeMoss Wolgemuth

Do not be anxious about anything, but in every situation, by prayer and petition, with thanksgiving, present your requests to God.

(Philippians 4:6)

Maundy Thursday, 16/4/87.

Last supper, upper room.   JIM HAMILTON:

All the following came from one evening spent ~~with~~ by:
Jesus with the disciples :

John 13 - the secret of joy
    (see vv 12-20 and 34-36). Servanthood.

John 14 - the provision of peace
    (v. 27) Jesus gave it there & then.

John 15 - the assurance in abiding
    (vv 4-9) We will bear fruit.

John 16 - the promise of ~~peace~~ power.
    (vv 7+12) In the Spirit.

John 17 - the essence of unity.
    (vv 20+21 +19).

"[SUFFERING] BRINGS OUT GRACES THAT CANNOT BE SEEN IN A TIME OF HEALTH. IT IS THE TREADING OF THE GRAPES THAT BRINGS OUT THE SWEET JUICES OF THE VINE; SO IT IS AFFLICTION THAT DRAWS FORTH SUBMISSION, WEANEDNESS FROM THE WORLD, AND COMPLETE REST IN GOD. USE AFFLICTIONS WHILE YOU HAVE THEM."

Robert Murray McCheyne

Not only so, but we also glory in our sufferings, because we know that suffering produces perseverance; perseverance, character; and character, hope.

(Romans 5:3-4)

"THE WEAKER I AM, THE HARDER I MUST LEAN ON GOD'S GRACE; THE HARDER I LEAN ON HIM, THE STRONGER I DISCOVER HIM TO BE, AND THE BOLDER MY TESTIMONY TO HIS GRACE."

Joni Eareckson Tada

That is why, for Christ's sake, I delight in weaknesses, in insults, in hardships, in persecutions, in difficulties. For when I am weak, then I am strong.

(2 Corinthians 12:10)

SUFFERING, COMFORT AND CONTENTMENT

"THE WORD COMFORT IS FROM TWO LATIN WORDS MEANING 'WITH' AND 'STRONG' - HE IS WITH US TO MAKE US STRONG. COMFORT IS NOT SOFT, WEAKENING COMMISERATION, IT IS TRUE, STRENGTHENING LOVE."

Amy Carmichael

For just as we share abundantly in the sufferings of Christ, so also our comfort abounds through Christ.

(2 Corinthians 1:5)

"YOUR
FAITH WILL
NOT FAIL WHILE
GOD SUSTAINS IT;
YOU ARE NOT STRONG
ENOUGH TO FALL AWAY
WHILE GOD IS RESOLVED
TO HOLD YOU."

J.I. Packer

Cast your cares on the LORD and
he will sustain you; he will
never let the righteous be
shaken.

(Psalm 55:22)

"TO FEAR IS TO HAVE MORE FAITH IN YOUR ANTAGONIST THAN IN CHRIST."

D. L. Moody

Cast all your anxiety on him because he cares for you. Be alert and of sober mind. Your enemy the devil prowls around like a roaring lion looking for someone to devour. Resist him, standing firm in the faith, because you know that the family of believers throughout the world is undergoing the same kind of sufferings.

(1 Peter 5:7-9)

"THE CHURCH
IS A HOSPITAL
FOR SINNERS,
NOT A MUSEUM
FOR SAINTS."

Timothy Keller

Dear children, let us not love
with words or speech but with
actions and in truth.

(1 John 3:18)

"HERE ARE WONDERS UPON WONDERS: THE STRONG ONE IS WEAK; THE INFINITE ONE LIES IN A MANGER; THE PRINCE OF LIFE DIES; THE CRUCIFIED ONE LIVES; THE HUMILIATED ONE IS GLORIFIED.

MEEKNESS AND MAJESTY, INDEED! BEHOLD, THEN, YOUR NEWBORN KING! COME AND WORSHIP HIM!"

Sinclair B. Ferguson

The Word became flesh and made his dwelling among us. We have seen his glory, the glory of the one and only Son, who came from the Father, full of grace and truth.

(John 1:14)

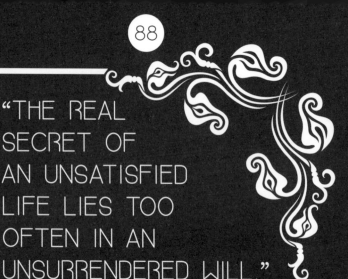

"THE REAL
SECRET OF
AN UNSATISFIED
LIFE LIES TOO
OFTEN IN AN
UNSURRENDERED WILL."

James Hudson Taylor

I appeal to you therefore, brothers, by
the mercies of God, to present your
bodies as a living sacrifice, holy
and acceptable to God, which
is your spiritual worship.

(Romans 12:1 ESV)

"LET US NEVER FORGET THAT WHAT WE ARE IS MORE IMPORTANT THAN WHAT WE DO."

James Hudson Taylor

I am crucified with Christ: nevertheless I live; yet not I, but Christ liveth in me: and the life which I now live in the flesh I live by the faith of the Son of God, who loved me, and gave himself for me.

(Galatians 2:20 KJV)

"WORRY DOES NOT
EMPTY TOMORROW
OF ITS SORROW,
IT EMPTIES TODAY
OF ITS STRENGTH."

Corrie ten Boom

Therefore do not worry
about tomorrow, for
tomorrow will worry about
itself. Each day has enough
trouble of its own.

(Matthew 6:34)

"FORGIVENESS IS THE KEY THAT UNLOCKS THE DOOR OF RESENTMENT AND THE HANDCUFFS OF HATRED. IT IS A POWER THAT BREAKS THE CHAINS OF BITTERNESS AND THE SHACKLES OF SELFISHNESS."

Corrie ten Boom

Bear with each other and forgive one another if any of you has a grievance against someone. Forgive as the Lord forgave you.

(Colossians 3:13)

THE
BIBLE

"A KNOWLEDGE OF THE BIBLE IS ESSENTIAL TO A RICH AND MEANINGFUL LIFE. FOR THE WORDS OF THIS BOOK HAVE A WAY OF FILLING IN THE MISSING PIECES, OF BRIDGING THE GAPS, OF TURNING THE TARNISHED COLORS OF OUR LIFE TO JEWEL-LIKE BRILLIANCE. LEARN TO TAKE EVERY PROBLEM TO THE BIBLE."

Billy Graham

All Scripture is God-breathed and is useful for teaching, rebuking, correcting and training in righteousness.

(2 Timothy 3:16)

"THE OBJECT OF THE BIBLE IS NOT TO TELL HOW GOOD MEN ARE, BUT HOW BAD MEN CAN BECOME GOOD."

D. L. Moody

For the word of God is alive and active. Sharper than any double-edged sword, it penetrates even to dividing soul and spirit, joints and marrow; it judges the thoughts and attitudes of the heart.

(Hebrews 4:12)

"BEGIN AT THE BEGINNING OF GENESIS, AND READ TO THE END OF THE REVELATIONS, AND SEE IF YOU CAN FIND, THAT THERE WERE EVER ANY THAT TRUSTED IN THE LORD, AND WERE CONFOUNDED."

John Bunyan

In that day they will say, "Surely this is our God; we trusted in him, and he saved us. This is the LORD, we trusted in him; let us rejoice and be glad in his salvation."

(Isaiah 25:9)

HEAVEN
AND
ETERNITY

"HEAVEN GIVES US HOPE—HOPE FOR TODAY AND HOPE FOR THE FUTURE. NO MATTER WHAT WE'RE FACING, WE KNOW IT IS ONLY TEMPORARY, AND AHEAD OF US IS HEAVEN."

Billy Graham

I consider that our present sufferings are not worth comparing with the glory that will be revealed in us.

(Romans 8:18)

"THIS IS THE COMFORT OF THE GODLY: THE GRAVE CANNOT HOLD THEM, AND THEY LIVE AS SOON AS THEY DIE.

FOR DEATH IS NO MORE THAN TURNING US OVER FROM TIME TO ETERNITY."

William Penn

When the perishable has been clothed with the imperishable, and the mortal with immortality, then the saying that is written will come true: "Death has been swallowed up in victory."

"Where, O death, is your victory?
Where, O death, is your sting?"

(1 Corinthians 15:54-55)

"SOME WANT TO LIVE WITHIN THE SOUND

OF CHURCH OR CHAPEL BELL;

I WANT TO RUN A RESCUE SHOP,

WITHIN A YARD OF HELL."

C.T. Studd

Rescue those being led away to death; hold back those staggering toward slaughter.

(Proverbs 24:11)

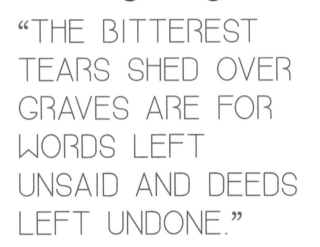

98

"THE BITTEREST TEARS SHED OVER GRAVES ARE FOR WORDS LEFT UNSAID AND DEEDS LEFT UNDONE."

Harriet Beecher Stowe

And let us consider how we may spur one another on toward love and good deeds.

(Hebrews 10:24)

"WE FOOLISH MORTALS SOMETIMES LIVE THROUGH YEARS NOT REALIZING HOW SHORT LIFE IS, AND THAT TODAY IS YOUR LIFE."

Edith Schaeffer

Why, you do not even know what will happen tomorrow. What is your life? You are a mist that appears for a little while and then vanishes.

(James 4:14)

"TAKE ALL AWAY. I AM CONTENT TO KNOW

SUCH LOVE IS MINE—FOR LIFE IS ALL TOO BRIEF

TO GRIEVE FOR PLEASURES BRINGING ONLY GRIEF;

GIVE ME BUT YOU; IT IS ENOUGH JUST SO."

Ruth Bell Graham

But he said to me, "My grace is sufficient for you, for my power is made perfect in weakness." Therefore I will boast all the more gladly about my weaknesses, so that Christ's power may rest on me.

(2 Corinthians 12:9)

101

"RESCUE THE PERISHING, CARE FOR THE DYING, SNATCH THEM IN PITY FROM SIN AND THE GRAVE; WEEP O'ER THE ERRING ONE, LIFT UP THE FALLEN, TELL THEM OF JESUS THE MIGHTY TO SAVE."

Fanny Crosby

Be merciful to those who doubt; save others by snatching them from the fire; to others show mercy, mixed with fear—hating even the clothing stained by corrupted flesh.

(Jude 1:22-23)

END
NOTES

LOVE

1.   D. L. Moody, *Prevailing Prayer: What Hinders It?* Diggory Press, 2007

2.   Ralph Erskine, *The Sermons and other Practical Works, R. Baynes, 1821*

3.   Shakespeare, William, *Shakespeare's Sonnets, The Complete Illustrated Edition*, Cider Mills Press, 2016

4.   Walter Scott, *The Lay of the Last Minstrel,* Birlinn; Bowhill Edition edition, 2013

5.   John Owen, *Communion with God, Christian Focus Publications, 2007*

6.   J.I. Packer, *Knowing God*, Hodder and Stoughton, 2005

7.   Watchman Nee, *The Spiritual Man (3 volume set)*, Christian Fellowship Publishers, Inc, 1968

8.   Charles Spurgeon, *The Soul Winner, Cosimo Classics, 2007*

9.   John Stott, *Bible Speaks Today commentary*, On 2 John. www.en.wikiquote.org/wiki/John_Stott

10.   Bernard of Clairvaux, *On Loving God, Cistercian Publications, 1937*

11. Andrew Murray, *With Christ in the School of Prayer*, Bridge Publishing, 1999

12. C. S. Lewis, *Letters of C.S. Lewis 1966*, Geoffrey Bles Ltd., London

13. Letters of C. S. Lewis (17 July 1953), *The Quotable Lewis*, Tyndale House Publishers, 2006

14. William Barclay, www.wmpl.org/quote/love-always-involves-responsibility

15. C. S. Lewis, *Mere Christianity*, William Collins, 2016

16. Catherine Booth, *The Love Letters of William and Catherine Booth, www.newfrontierchronicle.org*

17. G.K. Chesterton, *Illustrated London News*, 16 July 1910

18. *Victor Hugo, Les Misérables, Penguin Classics, 1982*

19. J.C. Ryle, *Expository Thoughts on the Gospels: John, Volume 3, Banner of Truth, 1982*

20. John Wesley, *Letter to Joseph Benson,* 7 November 1768, published in *The Letters of John Wesley, Hodder and Stoughton, 1915*

21. Jonathan Edwards, *Charity and its Fruits, Banner of Truth, 1982*

22. Alexander MacLaren, *Dictionary of Burning Words of Brilliant Writers*, W. B. Ketcham, 1895

23. William Gurnall, *The Christian in Complete Armour, Banner of Truth, 1964*

GOD AND CHRIST

24. Ravi Zacharias, *Jesus Among Other Gods: The Absolute Claims of the Christian Message*, Thomas Nelson, 2010

25. Isaac Watts Psalm 90, Stanza 1, "*Our God our help in ages past*",1719, www.bartleby.com

26. John Bunyan, *The Pilgrims Progress; From This World to That Which Is to Come, SCM, 1947*

27. Alistair Begg, *Made for his Pleasure*, Moody Press, 2005

28. Billy Graham, *The Heaven Answer Book*, Thomas Neilson, 2012

29. Jonathan Edwards, *The Life and Diary of David Brainerd, Cosimo Classics, 2007*

30. Matthew Henry, Matthew 22, *Matthew Henry's Concise Commentary on the Whole Bible, Thomas Nelson Inc, 2003*

31. Ligon Duncan, *Fear Not! Death and the Afterlife from a Christian Perspective*, Christian Focus Publications, 2010

SALVATION

32. Joseph Foulkes Winkes, edited by, *The Christian Pioneer*, University of Oxford, 1856

33. John Stott, *The Cross of Christ,* IVP, 2006

34. John Owen, *Overcoming Sin and Temptation*, Crossway Books, 2015

35. Matthew Henry, *The Life of the Rev. Philip Henry, A.M., Matthew Henry, J. B. Williams*, W. Ball, 1839

36. Thomas Brooks, *Smooth Stones Taken from Ancient Brooks* (1860), Kessinger Pub Co, 2009

37. Sinclair B. Ferguson, *In Christ Alone: Living the Gospel Centered Life,* Evangelical Press, 2008

38. Matt Chandler, *Creature of the Word: The Jesus-Centered Church*, B&H Books, 2012

39. Samuel Rutherford, as quoted by Joni Eareckson-Tada in *Heaven: Your Real Home*, Zondervan, 1995

40. Samuel Rutherford, *Letters* by Andrew Alexander Bonar, (Letter 56 to Lady Kenmure), Oliphant, Anderson & Ferrier, 1904

41. Martyn Lloyd-Jones, *Out of the Depths*, Christian Focus Publications, 2011

42. Martyn Lloyd-Jones, *Studies in the Sermon on the Mount*, IVP, 1977

43. Martyn Lloyd-Jones, *Studies in the Sermon on the Mount*, IVP, 1977

44. Elizabeth Barrett Browning, *No XXVI, Sonnets from the Portuguese* (1850), Doubleday, 1990

PRAYER

45. Martyn Lloyd-Jones, *Studies in the Sermon on the Mount*, IVP, 1977

46. Oswald Chambers, *My Utmost for His Highest Journal,* Barbour Pub Inc, 1997

47. R. C. Sproul, *The Prayer of the Lord,* Evangelical Press, 2009

48. Richard Bewes, *150 Pocket Thoughts*, Christian Focus Publications, 2004

49. A. W. Tozer, *The Pursuit of God,* Tate, 2013

50. Nancy DeMoss Wolgemuth, *A Place of Quiet Rest: Finding Intimacy With God Through a Daily Devotional Life*, Moody Publishers, 2002

51. Billy Graham, *Hope for Each Day Morning & Evening Devotions*, Thomas Nelson, 2012

52. F. B. Meyer, *Great Men of the Bible: Volume I*, Zondervan, 1981

53. E. M. Bounds, *Purpose in Prayer*, Whitaker House, 1997

54. John Piper, *Twitter stream (2009-11-09)*

LIFE AND FAITH

55. John Piper, *A Hunger for God: Desiring God through Fasting and Prayer*, Crossway Books, 1997

56. Hugh Latimer, *Hugh Latimer Sermons,* Cambridge University Press, 1844

57. John Bunyan, *The Pilgrim's Progress,* OUP Oxford, 2003

58. Thomas Brooks, *The Secret Key to Heaven (1665),* Banner of Truth, 2006

59. Timothy Keller, *Preaching: Communicating Faith in an Age of Skepticism*, Viking, 2015

60. Nancy Leigh DeMoss, *Choosing Gratitude: Your Journey to Joy*, Moody Publishers, 2011

61. A. W. Pink, *The Life of Elijah*, The Banner of Truth Trust, 1976

62. John Knox, www.goodreads.com/quotes

63. Elisabeth Elliot, *A Chance to Die: The Life and Legacy of Amy Carmichael*, Fleming H. Revell Co, 2005

64. Charles W. Colson, *God and Government: An Insider's View on the Boundaries Between Faith and Politics*, Zondervan, 2007

65. Augustine of Hippo, *The City of God*, Penguin Classics, 2003

66. E. M. Bounds, *Power Through Prayer*, Merchant Books, 2013

67. William Penn, www.*goodreads.com/author/quotes*

68. Martin Luther, www.*goodreads.com*

69. John Stott, *Basic Christianity*, IVP, 2013

70. R. C. Sproul, *Knowing Scripture*, IVP USA, 2009

71. Watchman Nee, *The Normal Christian Life*, Kingsway Publications, 1971

72. Watchman Nee, *The Normal Christian Life*, Kingsway Publications, 1971

73. Matthew Henry, Psalm 27:1, *Matthew Henry's Concise Commentary on the Whole Bible*, Thomas Nelson Inc, 2003

SUFFERING, COMFORT AND CONTENTMENT

74. Joni Eareckson Tada, *A Place of Healing: Wrestling with the Mysteries of Suffering, Pain, and God's Sovereignty*, David C Cook Publishing, 2016

75. Augustine of Hippo, *The City of God*, Penguin Classics, 2003

76. Augustine of Hippo, *Confessions*, Penguin Classics, 2015

77. Billy Graham, *Quotes from Billy Graham: A Legacy of Faith*, B&H Books, 2013

78. Isobel Kuhn, *By Searching: My Journey Through Doubt Into Faith*, Moody Publishers, 1959

79. Thabiti M. Anyabwile, *The Life of God in the Soul of the Church: The Root and Fruit of Spiritual Fellowship*, Christian Focus Publications, 2012

80. Nancy DeMoss Wolgemuth, *Choosing Gratitude: Your Journey to Joy*, Moody Publishers, 2011

81. Robert Murray McCheyne, *Comfort in Sorrow*, Christian Focus Publications, 2002

82. Joni Eareckson Tada, *God's Hand in Our Hardship*, Rose Publishing, 2014

83. Amy Carmichael, *Kohila: The Shaping of an Indian Nurse*, CLC Publications, 2002

84. J.I. Packer, *Knowing God*, Hodder and Stoughton, 2005

85. D. L. Moody, *The Overcoming Life,* Moody Publishers, 2010

86. Timothy Keller, *The Reason for God: Belief in an Age of Skepticism,* Hodder and Stoughton, 2009

87. Sinclair B. Ferguson, *In Christ Alone: Living the Gospel Centered Life*, Evangelical Press, 2008

88. James Hudson Taylor, *Union And Communion* or *Thoughts on the Song of Solomon,* Cosimo Classics, 2007

89. James Hudson Taylor, *Union And Communion* or *Thoughts on the Song of Solomon, Cosimo Classics, 2007*

90. Corrie ten Boom, *Clippings from My Notebook*, Triangle, 1983

91. Corrie ten Boom, *Clippings from My Notebook*, Triangle, 1983

BIBLE

92.   Billy Graham, www.billygraham.org.uk/devotion/
      know-the-bible, 04/06/2017

93.   D. L. Moody, *Pleasure And Profit In Bible Study And
      Anecdotes, Incidents And Illustrations*, Pomono
      Press, 2007

94.   John Bunyan, *Grace Abounding to the Chief of
      Sinners*, Echo Library, 2007

HEAVEN AND ETERNITY

95.   Billy Graham, *The Heaven Answer Book*, Thomas
      Nelson, 2012

96.   William Penn, www.*goodreads.com/quotes*

97.   C. T. Studd, www.*goodreads.com/quotes*

98.   Harriet Beecher Stowe, *Little Foxes: Or, the
      Insignificant Little Habits Which Mar Domestic
      Happiness*, Leopold Classic Library, 2015

99.   Edith Schaeffer, *The Hidden Art of Homemaking*,
      Tyndale House Publishers, 1974

100. Ruth Bell Graham, *Sitting by My Laughing Fire*,
      Wesscott Marketing, 2006

101. Fanny Crosby, *Rescue the perishing*, (1869),
      www.hymnary.org

Christian Focus Publications

Our mission statement –

STAYING FAITHFUL

In dependence upon God we seek to impact the world through literature faithful to His infallible Word, the Bible. Our aim is to ensure that the Lord Jesus Christ is presented as the only hope to obtain forgiveness of sin, live a useful life and look forward to heaven with Him.

Our books are published in four imprints:

CHRISTIAN FOCUS

Popular works including biographies, commentaries, basic doctrine and Christian living.

CHRISTIAN HERITAGE

Books representing some of the best material from the rich heritage of the church.

MENTOR

Books written at a level suitable for Bible College and seminary students, pastors, and other serious readers. The imprint includes commentaries, doctrinal studies, examination of current issues and church history.

CF4•K

Children's books for quality Bible teaching and for all age groups: Sunday school curriculum, puzzle and activity books; personal and family devotional titles, biographies and inspirational stories – because you are never too young to know Jesus!

Christian Focus Publications Ltd,
Geanies House, Fearn, Ross-shire,
IV20 1TW, Scotland, United Kingdom.
www.christianfocus.com